T0258304

RAT PACK CONFIDENTIAL

RAT PACK CONFIDENTIAL

by Shawn Levy

Adapted for the stage by
Paul Sirett

OBERON BOOKS
LONDON

This adaptation first published in 2002 by Oberon Books Ltd.
(incorporating Absolute Classics)
521 Caledonian Road, London N7 9RH
Tel: 020 7607 3637 / Fax: 020 7607 3629
e-mail: oberon.books@btinternet.com
www.oberonbooks.com

Rat Pack Confidential copyright © Shawn Levy 1998

Adaptation copyright © Paul Sirett 2002

Paul Sirett is hereby identified as author of this adaptation in accordance with section 77 of the Copyright, Designs and Patents Act 1988. The author has asserted his moral rights.

All rights whatsoever in this adaptation are strictly reserved and application for performance etc. should be made before commencement of rehearsal to Micheline Steinberg Playwrights Ltd, 4th Floor, 104 Great Portland Street, London W1W 6PE (e-mail SteinPlays@aol.com). No performance may be given unless a licence has been obtained, and no alterations may be made in the title or the text of the play without the author's prior written consent.

The individual copyrights for all songs included in the show remain with the respective publishers. Application to perform any of the songs listed here as part of *Rat Pack Confidential* should be made via Performing Rights Society before commencement of rehearsal. Authorisation is not guaranteed.

This book is sold subject to the condition that it shall not by way of trade or otherwise be circulated without the publisher's consent in any form of binding or cover other than that in which it is published and without a similar condition including this condition being imposed on any subsequent purchaser.

A catalogue record for this book is available from the British Library.

ISBN: 978-1-8400-2341-1

Cover image: De Facto Design

Characters

Announcer

JOEY
in his seventies

FRANK
in his forties

SAMMY
in his thirties

DEAN
in his forties

PETER
in his forties

Rat Pack Confidential was first performed at the Nottingham Playhouse on 6 September 2002, with the following cast:

FRANK SINATRA, Richard Shelton

DEAN MARTIN, Alex Giannini

PETER LAWFORD, Robin Kingsland

JOEY BISHOP, Alan Rothwell

SAMMY DAVIS Jr, Peter Landi

Director, Giles Croft

Designer, Mark Bailey

Choreographer, Sam Spencer Lane

Musical Director, John Morton

Lighting Designer, Jeanine Davies

Sound Designer, Paul Stear

Voice Coach, Sally Hague

Company and Stage Manager, Jane Eliot-Webb

Deputy Stage Manager, Anita Drabwell

List of Songs

TOGETHER WHEREVER WE GO (Styne/Sondheim)

WHEN YOU'RE SMILING (Fisher/Goodwin/Shay)

MEDLEY #1: THAT'S AMORE (Warren/Brooks); VOLARE (Modugno/Migliacci/Parish); COME FLY WITH ME (Van Heusen/Cahn); I'VE GOT YOU UNDER MY SKIN (Porter)

HIGH HOPES (Van Heusen/Cahn)

IN THE WEE SMALL HOURS OF THE MORNING (Mann/Hilliard)

I GET A KICK OUT OF YOU (Porter)

PENNIES FROM HEAVEN (Johnstone/Burke)

LET'S FACE THE MUSIC AND DANCE (Berlin)

GET HAPPY (Arlen/Koehler)

STRANGERS IN THE NIGHT (Kaemfert/Singleton/Snyder)

MEMORIES ARE MADE OF THIS (Gilkyson/Dehr/Miller)

WHAT KIND OF FOOL AM I? (Newley/Bricusse)

LITTLE OLE WINE DRINKER ME (Mills/Jennings)

MEDLEY #2: YOU MAKE ME FEEL SO YOUNG (Myrow/Gordon); SWAY (Ruiz/Gimbel); HEY THERE (Adler/Ross); THE LADY IS A TRAMP (Rodgers/Hart); EVERYBODY LOVES SOMEBODY (Taylor/Lane); ME AND MY SHADOW (Dreyer/Jolson/Rose)

MY WAY (François/Revaux/Thibaut/Anka)

THE BIRTH OF THE BLUES (Henderson/de Sylva/Brown)

A few of lines from: I LEFT MY HEART IN SAN FRANCISCO (Cory/Cross)

Note
The following script was correct at time of going to press but may differ slightly from the play as performed.

July 1998. A stage; a five-piece band, a microphone and microphone stand, a stool.

ANNOUNCER: Ladies and gentlemen…

A portentous timpani roll.

Would you please welcome the host of tonight's show, we're very lucky to have him… The one…the only… Mister Showbiz himself…you all know him…

Timpani build to a crescendo.

Mister Joeeeeeeeeeyyyyyyyy Bishop!

Band plays 'Birth of the Blues'. JOEY – in his late seventies – enters.

JOEY: Thank you… Thank you…

Band stops playing.

Thank you, ladies and gentlemen. I'd like to tell you what a great pleasure it is for me to be here. A friend of Frank's invited me – er, told me to come here… See Frank's still got a lot of very good friends who'd do anything for him. Real nice guys – with names like Dutch, Skinny, Lucky… This is, er, my first public engagement since Frank Sinatra passed away a couple of months ago. And, you know I can't shake the feeling that he's still out there somewhere watching over me. So I better be careful what I say… You want the truth about Frank? He was a great guy. And I mean that –

HECKLER: You better!

JOEY: I see we got the fan club in. (*Continuing his routine.*) Last time I saw Frank was about eighteen months ago.

But I talked to him by phone when I got news he was ill. I said to him, 'Frank you gotta get well 'cause I ain't worked since you got sick'... But to be serious for a minute: Frank, the Rat Pack, all that – it was about having fun, and illness isn't fun. Frank's gone. But I like to think he's in heaven now with the other guys, and they're up there singin' and foolin' around –

The HECKLER sings a line from 'The Birth of the Blues'.

Thanks, pal, don't call us –

The HECKLER continues to sing.

The audition's next door –

The HECKLER continues.

Would somebody get that guy a record contract?

The HECKLER stops singing.

(*Continuing.*) They may not be here with us any more, Frank, Dean, Sammy, Peter…but, hey, memories – we sure as hell got them. I gotta tell you, I remember one time I worked with Frank I kept the audience going twenty-five minutes overtime every night. Frank kept telling me, 'You're solid now – you're on your way.' I was seventy-two years old at the time –

HECKLER: Son of a gun!

JOEY: You wanna come up here and do this?

The HECKLER gets up and walks towards the stage.

Okay… C'mon up, c'mon…

The HECKLER gets up on stage. The Heckler is FRANK SINATRA in his prime, circa 1960. JOEY is in shock.

FRANK: Wassamatta, Charlie?

JOEY: Frank?

FRANK: Thought you might appreciate a little help.

JOEY: This isn't funny.

FRANK: That's what I'm trying to tell you.

JOEY: Is? I mean… Frank?

FRANK: What's eatin' you?

JOEY: You just died is what's eatin' me!

FRANK: You sure that's me you're talking about?

JOEY: But how! I mean –

FRANK: I was told to come here.

JOEY: Oh my God!

FRANK: Something like that.

JOEY goes to walk off; FRANK pulls him back.

Get back here. Relax. Take a deep breath… Better?
Good. Let's get in the groove.

JOEY: The groove? I'm nearly eighty years old.

FRANK: And I'm dead. Let's do something!

JOEY: What you wanna do – call some hookers?

FRANK: Later, maybe. Let's get the guys together.

JOEY: You wanna get…?

FRANK: It'll be a gasser. (*To audience.*) Ladies and
gentlemen, would you please put your hands together for
the inimitable, Mr Sammy Davis Junior!

*A man enters from the wings. It is SAMMY DAVIS Jr circa
1960.*

SAMMY Hey, hey, hey! What's happenin'?

FRANK: I died.

SAMMY Frank! You mean? Even you!

FRANK: Even me.

SAMMY: So was it you summoned me here?

FRANK: I guess.

SAMMY: Just like the old days. (*Indicating JOEY.*) He okay?

FRANK: Sure.

SAMMY: So what's the scene?

FRANK: I thought maybe we could do something. A coupla numbers. Whatever.

SAMMY: Let's do it! – Hey! Hold it! Where's Dean?

FRANK: Where'd you think?

SAMMY: Shall I?

FRANK: Well if you don't, I will.

SAMMY: (*To audience.*) Ladies and gentlemen, a very, very fine entertainer, would you please welcome, direct from the bar – Mr Dean Martin!

DEAN MARTIN – also in his 1960 prime – enters from the door at the rear of the stalls, clutching a drink.

DEAN: (*Stopping to observe the audience as he makes his way to the stage.*) What are all these people doing in my room?

FRANK: Get up here!

DEAN: Well if it isn't…

DEAN gets up on stage.

(*To JOEY.*) You look like you could use a salad, pallie. (*To SAMMY.*) So what is this?

SAMMY: Frank's idea.

DEAN What is?

SAMMY: We're gonna do a show.

DEAN: Oh no.

FRANK: Ah, come on, Charlie. Why not?

DEAN: I'm tired.

FRANK: You're dead. How can you be tired?

SAMMY: I know! (*Calling to Band.*) Nelson!

Music cue: 'Together'.

JOEY: Nelson Riddle is here?

A man in the stalls jumps up. He is PETER LAWFORD, circa 1960.

PETER Wait! Hold it! Hold it! What about me!

FRANK: How'd Lawford get in here?

DEAN: Don't look at me.

SAMMY: He was one of us.

FRANK: That fink!

PETER Frank... Please... For old time's sake...

FRANK: I ain't talking to that English bum!

PETER: I'm sorry, Frank. I'm so sorry. Please forgive me.

SAMMY: Frank... All for one... C'mon...

FRANK: (*Thinks about it, then.*) Ah, let's get on with it.

PETER dashes up on stage.

PETER: Oh, thank you, Frank, thank you –

FRANK: Don't push it, Charlie!

SAMMY: We're together again – can you believe that?

DEAN: Oh, I'm all choked up.

FRANK: Sure.

Song: 'Together'.

FRANK, DEAN, SAMMY and PETER sing the first six lines together. Then they take lines separately. At the line, 'No egos,' JOEY exclaims.

JOEY: No egos!

The song continues. They coax JOEY into the routine. They all sing together. At the end of the chorus SAMMY starts to dance. FRANK grabs him.

FRANK: Not yet, Charlie.

The song continues. DEAN has trouble remembering a line. At 'They'll smack us with scallions,' FRANK shouts.

They'll smack you.

The song continues. At the end of the next chorus SAMMY starts to dance. FRANK grabs him.

Not yet, Charlie.

The song continues. FRANK and DEAN hum in harmony. JOEY interjects.

JOEY: What is this – the Everley brothers?

FRANK croons like Bing Crosby. JOEY interjects again.

Don't you BOO-BOO me!

Likewise, at the line about 'sharing romances', sung by DEAN.

What's he mean – share?

PETER: I gave all my old telephone numbers to Jack Kennedy.

FRANK: I say you could mention him?

SAMMY: He was gonna come up sooner or later.

PETER: I was his brother-in-law, after all.

FRANK: Don't remind me. (*Sings – taking out his wallet.*) Finances.

JOEY: Wanna buy a coupla points in a casino?

DEAN: I hear the Cal-Neva's for sale.

FRANK: Don't!

The song continues. They all song together. They come to the names.

SAMMY: Inseparable that's me, Sammy –

FRANK: And Frank –

DEAN: And Dean –

JOEY: And me, Joey –

PETER: (*Spoken.*) And Peter –

They all sing together. Then.

FRANK: (*To SAMMY.*) Now, Smokey, now!

SAMMY dances. PETER joins him in the routine.

They sing the finale together.

Song finishes. They freeze in position for the applause.

(*To audience.*) Ladies and Gentlemen we are honoured this evening to have some celebrities in our midst and, er, I'd like to introduce you now to a very beautiful young lady sitting just down here in front of us: Marilyn Monroe.

They identify a woman in the audience.

PETER: Marilyn, how are you?

SAMMY: Oh baby!

FRANK: Doesn't she look good, good, good!

DEAN: She sure does, does does!

FRANK: So beautiful. And, ladies and gentlemen, we also have with us tonight, would you please welcome the fabulous Tony Curtis and Janet Leigh. Tony, where are you?

SAMMY: There he is. Tony, baby!

DEAN: And sitting just over there, the gorgeous Judy Campbell, ladies and gentlemen. Judy Campbell. Who's that she's with, Frank?

FRANK: Don't ask. Judy! …And we are also much humbled –

DEAN: Oh, much, much humbled.

FRANK: To have with us a man who I'm sure we all of us respect and admire – Joseph P Kennedy, ladies and gentlemen. Joe Kennedy!

FRANK leaves the stage to shake the hand of a member of the audience. He then returns to the stage.

DEAN: And right at the back, ladies and gentlemen… Mr Sam Giancana! Momo baby!

Someone jumps up in the back row of the stalls and runs out. Shouts and gunshots are heard in the foyer.

That's Sam.

FRANK: Ladies and gentlemen, we're gonna leave you now in the very capable hands of one of our finest comics – Mister Joey Bishop.

JOEY: Frank!

FRANK, SAMMY, DEAN and PETER exit.

JOEY: (*To audience – uncertain.*) That was... I...

FRANK: (*From wings.*) Get on with it!

JOEY: (*To audience.*) There's, er... There's a lot been said about the Summit and the depraved behaviour of the so-called Rat Pack. I wanna put the record straight – It's all true... La Dolce Vita nothing: this bunch made Nero look like a Cub Scout. I couldn't keep up with those guys. I mean, I'm no angel –

DEAN: (*From wings.*) I am!

FRANK/SAMMY/PETER: (*From wings.*) Me too!

JOEY: (*Growing in confidence.*) Lemme tell you about the Summit. Picture this: The Sands Hotel, Las Vegas, 1960. A gig; a movie; a party; a floating crap game; a hustle; a joke...This was Frank's baby –

FRANK: (*From wings.*) Prove it!

JOEY: And what a gig! It was never the same thing twice, but it would most of the time go something like this: I'd do some stuff, then, Dean, say, would be introduced by me: 'And now, direct from the bar...'

Music cue: 'When You're Smiling'.

DEAN enters.

JOEY: (*To audience.*) Mr Dean Martin!

DEAN: How long I been on?

Song: 'When You're Smiling'.

DEAN sings. JOEY and PETER ad lib comments.

Song finishes.

JOEY: (*To audience.*) Dean Martin was one of the richest men in Hollywood. Which was quite something when you consider he couldn't add up –

DEAN: Whaddayamean – couldn't add up?

JOEY: There was this band leader from Cleveland that Dean worked for, name of Watkins.

DEAN: Aw now, they don't wanna know about that.

JOEY: Dean wanted out of his contract. After rehearsal one day, Watkins calls him over… (*As Watkins.*) Crocetti! Crocetti, get over here!

DEAN: Mr Watkins…

JOEY: (*As Watkins.*) What's this I hear about you got a gig at the Riobamba?

DEAN: It's a big break for me.

JOEY: (*As Watkins.*) You ain't doin' it.

DEAN: But –

JOEY: (*As Watkins.*) You got a contract!

DEAN: It's the Riobamba.

JOEY: (*As Watkins.*) I don't care it's the Rio Grande! You got a contract!

DEAN: What I gotta do?

JOEY: (*As Watkins.*) Do? What you gotta do is honour your contract.

DEAN: To get out the contract.

JOEY: (*As Watkins.*) Freedom of contract? You want – okay. Twenty per cent of your income for the next ten years.

DEAN: Ten per cent over five years.

JOEY: (*As Watkins.*) Seven years.

DEAN: Done.

FRANK enters. He is playing an agent.

FRANK: (*As Agent.*) Ten per cent.

DEAN: Ten per cent.

FRANK: (*As Agent.*) Who got you the Riobamba?

DEAN: You did.

FRANK: (*As Agent.*) Goddam right, I did! You tell me – do I do this for love? Do I do this for fun? No. I do this cos it's my goddam job! Ten per cent. Or no gig.

DEAN: Ten per cent.

SAMMY enters as Tony – a pal from Steubenville.

SAMMY: (*As Tony.*) Dino!

DEAN: Why if it isn't…

SAMMY: (*As Tony.*) Tony. All the way from Steubenville. See my old buddy, the Italian boy singer from Cleveland. So, how's it…?

DEAN: Good.

SAMMY: (*As Tony.*) 'Good'! You're a goddam star! 'Good'! New York! You shit! You must be… Got a license to print money. No?

DEAN: I'm broke.

SAMMY: (*As Tony.*) You need…? Here… (*Takes out some money.*) Take it.

DEAN: Nah.

SAMMY: (*As Tony.*) Two hundred dollars. Take it. Two hundred dollars. Ready cash.

DEAN goes to take the money. SAMMY retracts it.

(*As Tony.*) All I'm askin'…is a twenty per cent piece. As your manager.

DEAN: Twenty per cent.

DEAN takes the money and begins to count it. PETER enters and taps DEAN on the shoulder – he is playing another agent.

PETER: (*As Agent.*) I hear you say you were broke?

DEAN: Somethin' like that.

PETER: (*As Agent.*) Ever think what a top agent could do for you? Top money. Top dates. Radio. Hollywood.

DEAN: Sounds good –

PETER: (*As Agent.*) Let me tell you a story. Guy comes up to me, says, 'I've got talent.' 'So, you've got talent,' I say, 'what am I supposed to do?' 'I've got to prove my talent,' says he. 'So prove it,' says I. 'Can't,' says he. 'Why?' says I. 'Got no money to eat,' says he. 'What do you need?' says I. 'Fifty dollars,' says he. I give him fifty dollars. Know this fella's name? John Wayne.

DEAN: No!

PETER: (*As Agent.*) John Wayne. (*Takes out some cash.*) I'm oiling the wheels.

DEAN: That's a lot of money.

PETER: (*As Agent.*) That's a lot a talent. Thirty-five per cent. All I'm asking.

DEAN takes the money. JOEY – as Lou Costello – grabs DEAN.

JOEY: (*As Lou.*) Dino!

DEAN: Hey Louie!

JOEY: (*As Lou.*) How you doin'?

DEAN: Ah, you know.

JOEY: (*As Lou.*) I don't know. What's the 'you know'?

DEAN: I gotta get a nose job. You think I need a nose job?

JOEY: (*As Lou.*) You need a nose job.

DEAN: Big schnozzola.

JOEY: (*As Lou.*) King schnozzola.

DEAN: I need something more aquiline. Only I owe…

JOEY takes out some money.

JOEY: (*As Lou.*) It's yours.

DEAN: You wanna slice?

JOEY: (*As Lou.*) Of your schnozzola? Kiddin' you. Seeing it's you…twenty per cent.

FRANK taps DEAN on the shoulder. FRANK is playing an MD.

FRANK: (*As MD.*) You got a good voice there, kid.

DEAN: I do?

FRANK: (*As MD.*) As your respected Musical Director, I know these things.

DEAN: Why, thank you.

FRANK: (*As MD.*) No problem. You could really go places.

DEAN: I had the backin'…

FRANK takes out some cash.

FRANK: (*As MD.*) This make things a little easier?

DEAN: (*Taking the money.*) Sure does.

FRANK: (*As MD.*) I'll need…

DEAN: How's ten per cent sound?

FRANK: (*As MD.*) Ten per cent sounds just dandy.

JOEY: (*To audience.*) Add it up…a hundred and five per cent. For every dollar Dean Martin earned, he was out a nickel. Except, of course, that being Dean Martin, he never actually bothered to pay anybody back.

Music cue: Medley.

DEAN sings 'That's Amore'.

From that number the music goes straight into 'Volare', which DEAN also sings.

The music continues behind the following exchange.

FRANK: You had it easy. I had to work for every cent!

DEAN: Sure you did.

FRANK: Hey, in '39 I was earning fifteen dollars a week waiting tables at the Rustic Cabin, by the end of the war I'd grossed eleven million dollars. Me. I did it.

DEAN: I made money, Frank.

FRANK: But I made the most.

DEAN: You sure about that?

FRANK: Casinos, restaurants, land, films, TV –

DEAN: Me too.

FRANK: When I'd had it with Capitol – what I do? I get my own record label. And who'd I sign? You guys. And when I sell up, how much do I make? A cool million. (*Takes out a cheque and waves it around.*) Now that's what I call pocket money.

The Medley moves into 'Come Fly With Me', which FRANK then sings.

The music continues under the following.

DEAN: I ever tell you, Frank, I was earning two hundred and eighty-three thousand dollars a week on my NBC show.

FRANK: I ever tell you, Dean, I made five hundred thousand more than you from our co-production of *Four for Texas?* Every dollar you made I made two, three, four. You have an entourage of four; I have an entourage of eight.

JOEY: That include your hairpiece handler?

FRANK: This... This is the thanks I get! I got you parts in my films, I cut you deals. (*To PETER.*) I made you half a million on your ten thousand dollar investment in *Ocean's 11. (To DEAN.)* I paid you a hundred and fifty thousand on that movie.

SAMMY: A hundred and fifty thousand? You only paid me a hundred and twenty-five.

JOEY: A hundred and twenty-five! I worked for scale!

SAMMY: You paid Dean a hundred and fifty thousand?

FRANK: Would you – For a wedding present I give this guy profit participation in *Sergeant's 3* puts him on a par with me and Dean, and he's crowing about a measly twenty-five.

The Medley moves into 'I Got You Under My Skin', which SAMMY sings.

The others join in on the repeats at the end, PETER taking a line, then DEAN, before JOEY sings the final 'I got you' and all but FRANK sing the final 'Under my skin'.

Medley finishes.

SAMMY: Hey, Charlie Snob. Beat some time for me.

PETER claps out a rhythm – SAMMY goes into a tap routine.

JOEY: There's a great act folks – one guy dances, the other guy applauds. Headed for the big time, woo hoo!

SAMMY: Ah, leaves us alone would you, Joey. (*To PETER.*) Go ahead, beat some, buddy!

FRANK: Hurry up, Sam, the watermelon's getting warm.

SAMMY stops dancing.

SAMMY: Don't do that shit, Frank.

FRANK: Ah, why don't you be yourself and eat some ribs?

SAMMY: Frank –

FRANK: Keep smiling so the folks can see you, Smokey.

SAMMY: Frank, I hate that shit.

FRANK: It cracks you up.

SAMMY: All my life I had to put up with that.

JOEY: (*To audience.*) For years when Sammy played Vegas he wasn't allowed to walk through or even see the casino. Fact was; he wasn't allowed in any public areas – except when he was on stage, of course. And he couldn't stay at the hotel; they put him up in a shack on the other side of town. When he was in the army –

PETER: Hold it!

Music cue: 'High Hopes'.

PETER grabs a couple of buckets from off stage – he puts one on his head and passes the other to DEAN. They each grab a broom and a mop, which they use as rifles. PETER is playing the Captain. DEAN is playing the Soldier.

(*As Captain, to SAMMY.*) Attention!

SAMMY stands to attention.

Song: 'High Hopes'.

While FRANK sings the first verse, PETER circles SAMMY menacingly.

All but SAMMY sing the chorus.

FRANK sings the next verse, with the other three taking the 'rubber tree plant' line together.

The music continues under the following.

(*As Captain, to SAMMY.*) This area over here is 'Whites Only'. You do not cross this line. Understand? UNDERSTAND!

SAMMY: Yes, sir!

PETER: (*As Captain.*) Good.

PETER stands on the 'Whites Only' side of the line.

(*As Captain, to SAMMY.*) You! Soldier! Over here!

SAMMY: But –

PETER: (*As Captain.*) That's an order!

SAMMY crosses the line.

(*As Captain.*) This area is 'Whites Only'!

SAMMY: But you –

PETER: (*As Captain.*) Don't answer back!

SAMMY turns to go back.

(*As Captain.*) Halt! Where are you going!

SAMMY: Sir –

PETER: (*As Captain.*) Get back here!

SAMMY turns back.

(*As Captain.*) This area is 'White's Only'!

SAMMY turns again.

(*As Captain.*) Get back here!

The song continues, with FRANK singing the next verse.

While he sings, DEAN and PETER shove SAMMY back and forth.

Then SAMMY lashes out. They fight.

FRANK, DEAN, JOEY and PETER sing the chorus.

SAMMY ends up sprawled across the floor.

SAMMY: (*Spoken.*) You bust my nose!

The music continues under the following.

DEAN: (*As Soldier.*) Thirsty, buddy?

SAMMY: Yeh…I guess.

DEAN hands him a bottle of beer.

DEAN: (*As Soldier.*) There you go.

SAMMY: I… What is it?

DEAN: (*As Soldier.*) Beer.

SAMMY goes to drink. Stops. Thinks about it. Sniffs the bottle.

SAMMY: This smells like…

DEAN: (*As Soldier.*) Beer.

SAMMY: Urine.

DEAN: (*As Soldier.*) Can get that tang, you know. Specially that, you know, what they brew round here.

PETER: (*As Captain.*) Yeh. Drink.

SAMMY: Thanks, but –

PETER: (*As Captain.*) You ungrateful son of a bitch!

PETER and DEAN scuffle with SAMMY. PETER succeeds in tipping the contents of the bottle over SAMMY'S head. SAMMY sits there – drenched.

FRANK, DEAN, PETER and JOEY sing the chorus.

FRANK takes the verse, with the other three taking the 'rubber tree plant' line again.

While the music continues, SAMMY is held by DEAN. PETER has a can of white paint and a paint brush.

(*As Captain.*) I had an idea. Solve the problem of all this integration bullshit.

PETER paints SAMMY'S face white. SAMMY loses it – he lunges at PETER and DEAN. They fight. PETER and DEAN get the better of him and give him a beating. FRANK helps SAMMY to his feet.

SAMMY: My nose… They bust my – They bust it again!

FRANK carries on singing.

Song finishes.

JOEY throws SAMMY a white towel. DEAN exits.

FRANK: You can't give him a white towel. Go get him a brown towel.

SAMMY: Please, Frank. Enough.

JOEY: Is it any wonder he turned to Judaism?

SAMMY: You got a problem with that – Gottlieb!

JOEY: Hey, Bishop's a good Jewish name.

DEAN re-enters pushing a bar cart. PETER surreptitiously chops up some cocaine. He passes a couple of pills to SAMMY. SAMMY pops the pills.

DEAN: I don't know about you guys, but I need a salad.
(*Fixes himself a drink – to audience.*) You know, in truth,
this is only a gag. I don't drink anymore. I freeze it now
and eat it like a popsicle.

JOEY: Why don't you tell 'em how the boozing evolved
from a stage joke into the real thing, and how you started
to supplement it with a Percodin habit?

FRANK: Hey, Joey, c'mon...

PETER snorts some cocaine.

DEAN: (*Indicating PETER and SAMMY.*) Least I never got
into the kinda shit those two got into.

SAMMY: I wasn't so bad.

DEAN: What! One night you got so ripped on hash
brownies, you walked on stage, did one song, turned to
the audience and said...

SAMMY: (*To audience – stoned.*) Thank you and good night.

SAMMY goes to walk off; DEAN hauls him back on.

DEAN: You thought you'd done a whole show.

PETER laughs.

SAMMY: What you laughing at, Charlie? You was in and
out of rehab like a goddam yo-yo.

PETER: At least I tried to do something about it.

SAMMY: Excuse me! When you were doing detox at the
Betty Ford Clinic, you hired a helicopter to meet you out
in the desert so you could get high on cocaine.

JOEY: Now that's what I call resourceful.

SAMMY: You were always getting high and chasing skirt.

PETER: And you weren't?

SAMMY: I wouldn't have fooled around like you if I'd been married to Pat Kennedy.

FRANK: I don't know what she saw in the creep.

PETER: You may have forgotten this, but I was a movie star long before I met Pat.

FRANK: Movie star?

PETER: I got my first full contract with MGM when I was just twenty years old.

FRANK: You were an English pretty-boy B-movie actor.

PETER: I was in some great movies! I sang, danced!

FRANK: Don't remind me.

PETER: And I slept with the most beautiful women in the world.

JOEY: (*To audience.*) Before, during and after his marriage to Pat Kennedy.

PETER: When a woman got married she had to accept the fact her husband would cheat. You know that.

JOEY: Hey, you can leave me outta this.

PETER: Everywhere we went, all these...actresses.

JOEY: (*To audience.*) Or models as they were known in New York. But Peter wasn't the only one. Frank liked to make love to three or four at the same time – whilst lying on the floor listening to his own records.

FRANK: I was real good to my girls. I gave them all parts in my movies.

JOEY: (*To audience.*) And Dean would stick it to any human he could!

DEAN: You know, I been thinking, and I was a good at the s–e–x. But in all honesty, I have to say my main interest was golf.

PETER: If I didn't want to get laid, I'd get a girl to do something else for me. Every night of my life.

SAMMY: It was there to be had. Any way we wanted it. Sex wasn't the point though, not for me. It was just…if you didn't want to be alone.

PETER: Boy, you musta hated being alone an awful lot!

SAMMY: What do you know! Charlie the goddam Seal! You dare to – some of the things you got up to!

PETER: We all got into stuff!

SAMMY: Bondage? Kinky role-play? Pain? (*Flicks PETER's face.*) Slaps to the face… (*Pulls at PETER's shirt.*) Razors to the nipples…

PETER: Leave me alone.

SAMMY: Maybe you should tell us about Marilyn?

PETER: I don't wanna talk about Marilyn!

SAMMY: Aw, he don't wanna talk about her.

PETER: Maybe you should tell us about that Swedish broad?

SAMMY: That was love!

PETER: Love?

SAMMY: Yeh! What's the matter, you never heard the word before?

FRANK: Love 'em and leave 'em.

JOEY: Oh-ho! The Leader has spoken. Humped and dumped.

DEAN: That go for Ava too?

FRANK: Ava... She...

DEAN grabs a cloth and ties it on his head like a headscarf. He puts on some dark glasses and does his best to look sultry.

FRANK: (*Staring forlornly at DEAN.*) Ava...

DEAN: (*As Ava, to PETER.*) Get me a drink would you, darling.

FRANK: Hey hey hey hey hey! Who's Harvey?

DEAN: (*As Ava.*) Mmm? Oh, this is Peter?

PETER: Pleased to meet you.

FRANK: Sounds like a fruit.

DEAN: (*As Ava.*) He's British.

FRANK: Bye, Peter.

DEAN: (*As Ava.*) We were just having a drink, Frank.

FRANK: (*To PETER.*) You starin' at? Creep! Huh? Get out!

PETER: You can't talk to me –

FRANK: You want your legs broken, you asshole! Cos you're gonna get 'em broken I ever see you again. So help me, I'll kill you!

DEAN: (*As AVA.*) Same old, same old.

FRANK: Shut up!

DEAN: (*As Ava.*) Ahhhh, wassa madda wid Fwankie?

FRANK: Let's get outta here.

DEAN: (*As Ava.*) What is your problem?

FRANK: I love you.

DEAN: (*As Ava.*) So get me drink.

FRANK: You don't need another drink.

DEAN: (*As Ava.*) Don't tell me what I 'need'.

FRANK: (*Grabbing DEAN's arm.*) C'mon.

DEAN: (*As Ava.*) Off!

FRANK: Drunk.

DEAN: (*As Ava.*) Creep.

FRANK: Whore.

DEAN: (*As Ava.*) Sicko.

FRANK: Snake.

DEAN: (*As Ava.*) Weasel.

FRANK: Jezebel.

DEAN: (*As Ava.*) Lightweight.

FRANK: Dumbass.

DEAN: (*As Ava.*) Sonofabitch.

FRANK: Bitchofabitch.

DEAN: (As Ava.) Sonofabitchofabitch.

FRANK: Whore.

DEAN: (*As Ava.*) You already said that!

FRANK: Screw you!

> *FRANK and DEAN neck passionately. JOEY takes out a notebook and starts scribbling into it.*
>
> (*Noticing JOEY.*) Hey! You! What the hell you doin'! What's that you're writing? You a journalist? Gimmie! Gimmie that you mother! You!

A chase ensues. JOEY hides. FRANK gives up and looks for DEAN.

Ava…Ava…where…Ava…

DEAN reappears – as himself. FRANK looks heartbroken.

Music cue: 'In the Wee Small Hours'.

SAMMY: C'mon, you're over her.

FRANK: I don't know if I'll ever…

As FRANK sings a back projection displays the names of the women the Rat Pack are known to have been involved with. The projection ends with the words: 'And a cast of thousands…'

Song: 'In the Wee Small Hours'.

FRANK sings.

While singing, he starts to swallow a bottle of pills. DEAN, SAMMY, JOEY and PETER stop him.

He sings some more.

Then he slashes at his wrists. He collapses. DEAN, SAMMY, JOEY and PETER gather around him.

Song finishes.

FRANK leaps to his feet.

FRANK: Hey, I was down, but I wasn't out.

SAMMY: (*As Bogart, to FRANK.*) They tell me you have a voice that makes girls faint. Make me faint.

FRANK: I'm taking the week off.

SAMMY: Hey, where was it… You, Bogie and the gang at the…?

FRANK: Desert Inn.

SAMMY: In walks Lauren Bacall…

JOEY: (*To audience.*) AKA Mrs Bogart.

SAMMY throws a napkin to PETER. PETER puts it on as a headscarf.

PETER: (*As Lauren Bacall.*) You look like a goddam Rat Pack.

SAMMY: I love that.

PETER removes the 'headscarf'.

FRANK: When Bogart died...Sheeesh...

JOEY: Didn't you propose to his widow, Frank?

FRANK: So what? Hey, you guys know what Joe Kennedy did, when Peter Lawford announced he was getting engaged to his daughter?

JOEY: Ah, ah, ah...

JOEY grabs a cloth and wraps it around SAMMY'S waist like a skirt.

(*Indicating SAMMY.*) Pat Kennedy.

FRANK: See – there was gossip...

PETER: Totally unsubstantiated.

FRANK: Rumours about...(*Whispers.*)...homosexuality... (*Mixes himself a drink.*) Say, Dean, you know how to make a fruit cordial?

DEAN: Why, Frank, just be nice to him.

FRANK: Old Joe was so worried... (*To the member of the audience identified earlier as Joe Kennedy.*) Joe why don't you tell 'em...? Joe?

FRANK goes into the audience.

(*To the member of the audience identified as Joe Kennedy.*) What exactly happened?

FRANK leans down – in order to assimilate the audience member whispering in his ear.

Joe said he got J Edgar Hoover to open up his store of confidential files...

FRANK leans back down to hear more.

Which showed that Charlie Snob was a well-known patron of Hollywood prostitutes.

FRANK slaps the audience member on the back.

Old Joe was delighted! Ain't that right, Joe? Not only was the prospective brother-in-Lawford not a fruit, he was a genuine, paid up, sonofabitch, whore-mongering, man after his own heart.

FRANK makes his way back on stage.

JOEY: (*To audience.*) Frank had been trying to get an 'in' with the Kennedy's for some time. Finally, he had the idea of hitting on Peter.

FRANK: Peter!

PETER: Frank, hello.

FRANK: I haven't seen you since...

PETER: Since you threatened to break my legs.

FRANK: Charlie, I'm sorry, I was dead wrong about that. Please say you forgive me.

PETER: Well, sure.

FRANK: I appreciate that. I've always admired your work, Peter. You got that something you know.

PETER: I do.

FRANK: Star quality. You know what I'm saying.

PETER: Coming from you Frank.

FRANK: Maybe I could even persuade you to… Nah…

PETER: What?

FRANK: Well… Nah…

PETER: What, Frank, what?

FRANK: I'm making a movie. You'd be perfect.

PETER: I would?

JOEY: (*To audience.*) Peter hadn't worked in six years.

FRANK: What do you say?

PETER: Twist my arm.

FRANK: I will.

> *Music cue: 'I Get A Kick Out Of You'.*

I can see we're gonna be great buddies me and you.

PETER: I'd like that.

> *Song: 'I Get A Kick Out Of You'. FRANK sings.*

> *After the first verse, PETER asks.*

You do?

> *Then FRANK sings the next verse – after which PETER asks.*

Really?

> *After the next four lines FRANK accuses PETER of not adoring him. PETER defends himself.*

But I do, Frank! I do!

> *As FRANK builds to the finale, PETER joins him on the repeats.*

> *Song finishes.*

JOEY: (*To audience.*) And Frank was 'in'.

FRANK: (*To PETER – indicating SAMMY.*) Aren't you gonna introduce me?

PETER: Er...of course... (*Introducing SAMMY.*) Frank – my wife, Pat Kennedy.

FRANK: A pleasure to meet you.

PETER: (*Indicating the member of the audience FRANK has just left.*) And, er, Joe Kennedy, my father-in-law, I think you already know?

FRANK: Sir.

PETER: (*Introducing FRANK to DEAN.*) Jack Kennedy.

FRANK: Jack.

DEAN: (*As JFK.*) Frank.

PETER: And, er... (*Introducing FRANK to JOEY.*) And Bobby.

FRANK: Bobby, good to meet you.

DEAN: (*As JFK.*) Peter's been telling me about this new movie you're... What's it –

FRANK: Ocean's Eleven. Gang of war vets hold up a bunch of casinos. We're shooting next winter in Vegas. Doing some live shows while we're out there – me, Sammy, Dean...some guy name of Lawford. At the Sands Hotel. Promises to be quite something.

DEAN: (*As JFK.*) Maybe I'll catch up with you out there?

FRANK: You do that.

DEAN: (*As JFK.*) I will.

FRANK: Perhaps I could interest you in some of the 'lively arts' while you're there.

DEAN: (*As JFK.*) You do that.

FRANK: I will.

SAMMY, DEAN and JOEY break out of their Kennedy characters.

JOEY: (*To audience.*) It was at the Summit, Frank introduced Jack Kennedy to Judy Campbell. (*To audience member identified as Judy Campbell.*) Judy? That's right, ain't it? (*To FRANK.*) Frank?

FRANK: I might've made my apartment available to them for a private lunch – yes.

JOEY: Yes – And by the time Kennedy left they were what you might call 'firm friends'.

SAMMY: That's right – Jeez! Kennedy was there, holding court at the Summit, digging the scene in the Copa Room. And, yeh, every show Jack attended Frank'd introduce him with a bunch of sugary bullshit-

FRANK: Whadayamean?

SAMMY: Jack Kennedy this, Jack Kennedy that, Jack Kennedy, Jack Kennedy, Jack Kennedy.

DEAN: What d'you say his name was?

SAMMY: And then the night before he left…Peter, do you remember?

PETER: I remember.

JOEY: Cue the music.

Music cue: 'Pennies From Heaven'.

SAMMY: We attended some party in a private room. Kennedy was there. Strictly inner-inner circle. Peter took me to one side…

PETER puts an arm around SAMMY and takes him to one side.

PETER: If you want to see what a million dollars in cash looks like, go into the next room; there's a brown leather satchel in the closet; open it. It's a gift from the hotel owners for Jack's presidential campaign.

JOEY: (*To audience.*) For 'hotel owners' read – the mob.

Song: 'Pennies from Heaven'. PETER sings. SAMMY throws in the following after the first verse.

SAMMY: I never went near it.

After the next verse, SAMMY interrupts again.

One million dollars – in cash!

JOEY: Mob money.

SAMMY: Then some guy tells me there are these four hookers scheduled to entertain Kennedy. So I get out of there. Some things you don't wanna know.

JOEY: You had a coupla points in the Sands, ain't that right, Frank?

PETER: He upped it to nine soon after.

FRANK: What you getting at? Dean bought himself a piece. You all signed long-term deals. The Sands was our home.

JOEY: Yeh, but we didn't own a slice like you guys. We didn't front for nobody.

FRANK: I didn't front for nobody.

PETER: Every hotel on the strip was owned by some group of gangsters.

DEAN: Not so as you could show it on paper.

SAMMY: The mob built Vegas, everyone knows that.

JOEY: And I bet I know where that million dollars came from – the Central States Pension Fund of the International Brotherhood of Teamsters. Mob play-money.

Back to the song: PETER sings the last line.

Song finishes.

Ain't that right, Frank?

FRANK: Can we stop all this mob hokum?

JOEY: Hokum? (*To audience.*) Sam? Sam Giancana out there?

FRANK: Drop it, Charlie.

DEAN: He left.

JOEY: Okay… You sure about that?

DEAN: I don't see him.

JOEY: Okay. (*To audience.*) Let me tell you about Cuba.

FRANK: I said, drop it.

JOEY: February 11, 1947, a Pan Am clipper lands in Havanna, Cuba. Among the gay throng, three well-dressed men stood apart.

PETER and DEAN stand either side of FRANK. PETER hands FRANK a briefcase.

Frank Sinatra and his two buddies, Joe and Rocco Fischetti – cousins of Al Capone and brothers of Charlie 'Trigger-Happy' Fischetti. Frank gave three excuses for the trip.

FRANK: I wanted to visit a few days with the boys.

JOEY: In Cuba?

FRANK: I wanted to find me some sunshine.

JOEY: Along with enough Italo-Americans to fill three dozen suites at the Nacional?

FRANK: Could I help it if these guys wanted to throw a party in my honour?

JOEY: (*To audience.*) The real reason was for Mafia bosses to pay fealty and talk business with deported mob boss, Lucky Luciano.

FRANK: Was not!

JOEY: Was too! One mob guy said of the meeting:

SAMMY: (*As hood.*) Lucky Luciano was very fond of Sinatra's singing, but, of course, our meeting had nothing to do with listening to him croon.

JOEY: Among items on agenda were:

DEAN: (*A hood.*) The importation of narcotics.

PETER: (*As hood.*) The takeover of Flamingo Hotel in Vegas.

DEAN: (*As hood.*) And the execution of Benny Siegel for embezzling construction funds.

JOEY: Agents from the Federal Bureau of Narcotics believed the briefcase Frank carried contained two million dollars in cash earmarked for…Lucky Luciano.

FRANK: Bullsh– I never knew Luciano!

JOEY: You were photographed on your hotel balcony, smiling with him.

FRANK: I was just passing!

JOEY: You were seen at his table, dining with him.

FRANK: I couldn't get away, it mighta caused a scene.

JOEY: You were seen in the bar drinking with him.

FRANK: I didn't want to offend.

JOEY takes out a silver cigarette case.

JOEY: Police found this cigarette case in Lucky Luciano's home in Naples. Can you read what's engraved here?

FRANK: 'To my dear pal Lucky from his friend…Frank Sinatra.' Okay so he was an acquaintance, but nothing more. And there was not two million dollars in that bag. I mean, come on! Picture me, skinny Frankie, lifting two million dollars in small bills. For the record, one thousand dollars in dollarbills weighs three pounds, which makes the load I am supposed to have carried six thousand pounds. I stepped off the plane in Havana with a small bag in which I carried my oils, sketching materials, and personal jewellery, which I never send with my regular luggage.

JOEY: Dollarbills?

SAMMY: Oils?

DEAN: Sketching materials?

JOEY: Lee Mortimer, a journalist on the New York Daily Mirror, referred to Frank in the paper as Frank 'Lucky' Sinatra.

PETER: (*Laughs.*) Frank 'Lucky' Sinatra!

FRANK decks PETER.

JOEY: Frank slugged Mortimer. Ended up in court.

FRANK: And you know what? When he died, I visited the cemetery where they buried him and I pissed on his grave.

JOEY: I bet that impressed your mob buddies.

FRANK: What are you – squeaky clean all of a sudden? Who was it entertained at the wedding of Sam Giancana's daughter?

JOEY: Like I had a choice! Concrete boots were no joke with that guy.

FRANK: Hypocrite!

JOEY: Hey, I wasn't the one give him a sapphire pinky friendship ring and got all upset when I hear he never wears it.

FRANK: He wore it!

JOEY: (*To audience.*) Ladies and Gentlemen, I'd like to tell you about a swell guy name of Sam Giancana... (*To DEAN.*) You absolutely sure he left?

DEAN: I think so.

JOEY: Sam Giancana, top man of the Chicago mob, first murder indictment at age 18. Who knows how many guys he killed or how many hits he sanctioned since then? Hobbies? Some people play golf, Giancana tortures people. What a guy!

JOEY tosses a cherry bomb under SAMMY's feet. It explodes. SAMMY jumps.

Sam used to like to toss cherry bombs under people's feet just for fun.

JOEY tosses a cherry bomb at PETER. It explodes. PETER jumps.

Frank used to join in.

JOEY and FRANK toss cherry bombs around. They double up with laughter.

FRANK: So, Sam, how's your bird?

JOEY: (*As Sam Giancana.*) Can't complain.

FRANK: What brings you to Florida?

JOEY: (*As Sam Giancana.*) Operation Mongoose.

FRANK: What's Operation Mongoose?

JOEY: (*As Sam Giancana.*) The CIA would like the Mafia to assassinate Fidel Castro.

FRANK laughs. JOEY's face remains serious. FRANK's laugh subsides.

FRANK: You're serious.

JOEY: (*As Sam Giancana.*) And we're gonna take 'em for every cent we can.

FRANK: Actually, I, er…I was wondering… See, I got this buddy –

JOEY: (*As Sam Giancana.*) Frank, a buddy of yours is a buddy of mine.

FRANK: Don't you think it would be a terrible shame if Senator Kennedy were unable to secure the Democratic nomination?

JOEY: (*As Sam Giancana.*) And if I were to borrow say fifty thousand dollars from the Teamsters Central States Pension Fund to ensure that such a terrible shame did not occur, do you think that maybe this could buy decent citizens such as ourselves a little security?

FRANK: I would think you could count on it.

JOEY: (*As Sam Giancana.*) Just one other thing – that good-looking broad Senator Kennedy has been seeing…

FRANK: Judy Campbell.

JOEY: (*As Sam Giancana.*) Maybe you'd like to introduce us?

Music cue: 'Let's Face the Music and Dance'.

FRANK goes into the audience and identifies a member of the audience as Judy Campbell. He escorts her up on to stage.

FRANK: (*Introducing JOEY.*) Sam, I'd like you to meet Judy Campbell.

Song: 'Let's Face the Music and Dance'.

SAMMY sings.

After the first verse, JOEY, as Sam Giancana, hands Judy' a bunch of yellow roses.

JOEY: (*As Sam Giancana.*) Judy – for you.

SAMMY sings again. Then, after the next verse.

PETER: Why, if it isn't Senator Kennedy.

DEAN, as JFK, hands Judy' some red roses.

DEAN: (*As JFK.*) Judy – for you.

SAMMY carries on singing.

JOEY and DEAN shower Judy' with gifts.

SAMMY sings the next verse.

Song finishes.

FRANK ushers Judy' back to her seat.

SAMMY: You believe that Kennedy guy? Always chasing skirt.

FRANK: He had a healthy appetite.
(*Sings – to the tune of 'High Hopes'.*)
Everyone wants to back, Jack,
Jack is on the right track.

SAMMY: Had us just where he wanted us. Wheel us out when it suited him, shut us out when it didn't.

FRANK: They were great times.

SAMMY: You call getting up on stage at the Democratic Convention and being booed by the Alabama and Mississippi delegation a 'great time'?

FRANK: Least Jack got the nomination.

SAMMY: Yeh and as soon as it became apparent he'd need the Southern vote to make the White House, it was bye-bye Sammy.

FRANK: Smokey, c'mon, it was more complicated than that.

JOEY: (*To audience.*) Her name was May Britt and she was a white, Swedish movie star. Sammy made the announcement in London.

JOEY – as May Britt – takes SAMMY's hand.

SAMMY: May and I would like to announce that we have decided to get married.

DEAN: (*As American journalist.*) Are you announcing it over here because you're afraid to do it at home?

PETER: (*As British journalist.*) How will people at home feel about this?

DEAN: (*As American journalist.*) Isn't this the first marriage between a Negro man and a blonde, white movie star?

PETER: (*As British journalist.*) What happens if you can't go home?

DEAN: (*As American journalist.*) How would Miss Britt feel if her kid turns out to be black – you know what I mean?

SAMMY: Buddy, I know exactly what you mean, and as far as our children are concerned it wouldn't matter to us, if they were white, brown or polka-dot!

FRANK: Didn't that British guy set up some kinda picket?

PETER: Mosely.

DEAN and PETER hold up placards reading: 'Go home, nigger.' and 'Sammy, back to the trees.'

SAMMY: That was nothing – when I got home…wedding date set, Frank to be best man…

More placards: 'Go back to the Congo, you kosher coon.' and 'What's the matter Sammy, can't you find a coloured girl?'

And one of the weirdest things…

JOEY wheels on a black toy dog. The dog has a swastika on its side; around its neck hangs a placard.

(*Takes the sign from the dog's neck and reads.*) 'I'm black too, Sammy, but I'm not a Jew.' Could someone please explain that to me?

FRANK: Don't let it get to you.

SAMMY: I had death threats, bags full of hate mail… (*Takes out a letter, reads.*) 'Dear Nigger Bastard, I see Frank Sinatra is going to be best man at your abortion. Well, it's good to know the kind of people supporting Kennedy before it's too late.' Signed, 'An ex-Kennedy vote.'

FRANK: What an asshole!

SAMMY: I knew the pressure you musta been under – my best man. You musta had eighty guys telling you, 'Don't be a fool, you've worked hard for Kennedy, now do you want to louse him up?' You musta been getting it from all sides.

FRANK: I was.

JOEY: (*To audience.*) Frank wasn't gonna let his buddy down. He always had time for Sammy, even when most white musicians wouldn't give the time of day to a black act. Sammy knew it was up to him.

SAMMY: (*On phone.*) Frank…

FRANK: (*On phone.*) Smokey, what can I do for you?

SAMMY: Bad news. We're gonna have to postpone the wedding.

FRANK: No!

SAMMY: We got a problem with the banquet room…and the rabbi's schedule…

FRANK: You're lying, Charlie.

SAMMY: Look, what the hell, it's best we postpone it 'til after the election.

FRANK: You don't have to do that.

SAMMY: I want to. All the talk.

FRANK: Screw the talk!

SAMMY: I know, but it's better this way.

FRANK: I'll be there whenever it is. You know that, don't you?

SAMMY: Yes.

FRANK: And you know that I'd never ask you to do a thing like this. Not your wedding, I'd never ask that!

SAMMY: That's why it's up to me to be saying it.

FRANK: You're a better man than I am, Charlie. I don't know if I could do this for you, or for anyone…

SAMMY: You've been doing it, haven't you?

They hang up.

JOEY: (*To audience.*) It worked. The heat was off. They got married after the election.

SAMMY: A proud husband –

JOEY: (*To audience.*) And a pregnant bride under the chuppah.

FRANK: And Jack Kennedy...in the White House!

Music cue: 'Get Happy'.

JOEY: Only after you and Joe Kennedy prevailed upon Sam Giancana to pull a few strings so that Illinois fell his way.

Song: 'Get Happy'. FRANK sings. Then the music continues under the following.

PETER: Giancana was forever taking the credit for Jack's victory.

JOEY: Do I detect a hint of jealousy?

PETER: Was it Giancana gave Jack tips on how to look good on TV? It wasn't by mistake that Jack came across as positive and confident and Nixon looked like some unshaven shyster.

FRANK sings the rest of the song.

Song finishes.

FRANK: And then...the Inaugural Eve Gala.

DEAN: Sorry, can't make it.

SAMMY: I was so excited. I was gonna be at the inauguration. Me and my beautiful wife. And I said to myself, Jeez! It can really happen. Despite all the odds, an uneducated kid from Harlem could work hard and get invited to the White House.

Phone rings – SAMMY answers.

SAMMY: (*On phone.*) Yeah.

JOEY: (*As Secretary, on phone.*) Mr Davis...Sammy...this is Evelyn Lincoln, Jack's personal secretary...the President has asked me to tell you that he doesn't want you present at his inauguration. There is a situation into which he is being forced and to fight it would be counterproductive to the goals he's set. He very much hopes you will understand.

SAMMY: ...I understand.

PETER: They talked the President into it, Smokey. They said:

JOEY: (*As Presidential Aide, to DEAN.*) Look, this is our first time out. Let's not do anything to screw up. We've got southern senators, bigoted congressmen. They see you as too liberal to start with. If we have Sammy here, is he going to bring his wife? We can't ask him not to bring her.

DEAN: (*As JFK.*) Okay, then dump it. Call Sam. He'll understand.

PETER: (*To SAMMY.*) You'll be interested to know that Bobby argued for you. He said:

JOEY: (*As BOBBY.*) That's bullshit! It's wrong! The man campaigned!

PETER: But he was overruled. He got so angry he walked out.

FRANK: That was some night. When Kennedy made his speech...

DEAN: (*As JFK.*) We're all indebted to a great friend – Frank Sinatra. Long before he could sing, he used to poll a Democratic precinct back in New Jersey. That precinct has grown to cover a country.

PETER: And the rest…don't stop…

DEAN: (*As JFK.*) A great deal of our praise and applause should also go to the co-producer, my brother-in-law Peter Lawford.

JOEY: (*To audience.*) Frank bought an ad in Variety to have Jack's remarks reprinted, and had them pressed into a record which he would play over and over. Photographs of the evening, along with virtually every note and letter Jack ever sent him, found their way – framed – into a Kennedy Room at Frank's Palm Springs house. A shrine.

FRANK: You got a problem with that?

JOEY: Me? No, Frank. Just saying.

FRANK: How many times you get invited to the White House?

PETER: I ever tell you about the little betting pool me and Jack set up with some of Jack's old buddies from Choate and Harvard? The object of the pool was to reward the first man to sleep with a woman other than his wife in the Lincoln Bedroom. Joey…

PETER wraps a tablecloth around JOEY as a skirt.

(*To DEAN – introducing JOEY.*) Hey, Jack! Like you to meet someone…

PETER whispers into DEAN's ear.

DEAN: (*As JFK.*) The Lincoln Bedroom?

PETER: Uh huh.

DEAN: (*As JFK.*) You son of a gun! I knew you'd be the one to win.

DEAN pays PETER. PETER shoves JOEY away.

(*As JFK.*) Peter, I gotta take a trip to the West Coast, any chance you can arrange some accommodation for me out there.

PETER: Leave it with me, Jack.

PETER picks up a phone.

(*On phone.*) Frank – it's Peter. The President is coming out on a West Coast visit in March, and he was wondering would you mind the imposition of a visit.

FRANK: (*On phone.*) Mind?

JOEY: (*To audience.*) This was gonna be Frank's greatest moment. He ordered a major reconstruction of his Palm Springs estate. The house was expanded, with the addition of a banquet room able to seat forty, and a Kennedy Room. Two cottages were built to house Secret Service agents. He had a communications centre installed – with five private phone lines, teletype equipment and enough cable to handle a full switchboard. He had a concrete heliport poured, and a towering flagpole erected. And he ordered a bronze plaque reading: 'John F Kennedy Slept Here.' Then...

DEAN: (*As JFK.*) Peter.

PETER: Yes, Jack?

DEAN: (*As JFK.*) I want you to call Frank, tell him we can't stay at his place.

PETER: But Frank expects you to stay there, and anything less than your presence is going to make it difficult for Charlie here to explain.

DEAN: (*As JFK.*) You can handle it, Peter, we'll take care of the Frank situation when we get to it.

PETER: (*On phone.*) Frank…it's, uh…well, I…

FRANK: (*On phone.*) What is it, Charlie?

PETER: The, er, Secret Service have nixed your estate as a presidential retreat because of its open location.

FRANK: …They what?

PETER: The president can't stay at a place with such an open –

FRANK: So where's he staying? Where's he staying!

PETER: …Bing…

FRANK: Bing?

PETER: Bing Crosby's estate. It backs up against the mountains; it's more secure –

FRANK: He's a goddam Republican!

PETER: I – I – I – I know –

FRANK: I'm gonna rip your head off, you fuckin' limey sonofabitch whore! I'm gonna break your fuckin' legs and feed your balls –

PETER places a hand over the earpiece of his phone – silencing FRANK who continues to mouth abuse.

JOEY: (*To audience.*) Frank lost it.

FRANK slams the phone down and starts smashing things up.

DEAN: (*As JFK.*) How'd Frank take the news?

PETER: Not very well.

JOEY: Hey, Frank, you'll have to get a new plaque made: 'JFK Almost Slept Here.'

FRANK chases JOEY.

Frank – Sorry, sorry, sorry, sorry, sorry…

FRANK relents.

PETER: I was the one who took the brunt of it…Frank seemed to think I was responsible for setting Jack up to stay at Bing's. (*To FRANK.*) But I wasn't, Frank. I didn't. It wasn't me… I'm sorry. Why wouldn't you take my phone calls? Why didn't you answer my letters?

FRANK turns his back on PETER.

SAMMY: Frank, about Peter –

FRANK: That Englishman is a bum!

JOEY: (*To audience.*) When Frank Jnr got kidnapped – Frank rang him then. First time in eighteen months. He wanted Peter to contact Bobby and get the FBI on the case. Soon as Peter'd spoken to Bobby, he rang Frank straight back…

PETER: (*On phone.*) Bobby said he'd do everything possible.

FRANK: (*On phone.*) Thank you.

JOEY: (*To audience.*) It was the last time they ever spoke to each other. One time, Peter even flew to Vegas to catch Frank at Caesar's Palace; after he'd been seated for a while, two goons showed up at the table…

SAMMY and JOEY approach PETER.

SAMMY: (*As Goon.*) Sir, I'm afraid we're gonna have to ask you to leave.

PETER: No, no, you don't understand –

JOEY: (*As Goon.*) Mr Sinatra would like you to vacate your seat.

PETER: There must be some mistake –

SAMMY: (*As Goon.*) Mr Sinatra insists.

JOEY: (*As Goon.*) Or there'll be no show.

SAMMY and JOEY move away.

PETER: Milt! MILT! Where's my manager!

DEAN: (*As Milt Ebbins.*) Peter, I'm here. What is it?

PETER: You got to talk to Frank for me, you gotta –

DEAN: (*As Ebbins.*) Okay, okay, okay. Keep a lid on it.

DEAN turns to FRANK.

(*As Ebbins.*) Frank, you can't do this to Peter.

FRANK: Oh, I can't?

DEAN: (*As Ebbins.*) You want the truth? Bobby didn't want Jack so close when so many of your pals were under such intense Justice Department scrutiny.

FRANK: That Englishman is a goddam bum!

JOEY: (*To audience.*) None of it worked. Frank just wrote Peter off. And Peter was destroyed. He loved Frank. He loved being a part of the Rat Pack. And all of a sudden he was on the outs… You want the truth of what happened? (*To MD.*) Maestro…

Music cue: 'Strangers in the Night'.

JOEY hauls a flip chart centre stage. Every now and then he hums or sings a line from the song.

Draws a male figure on one side of the flip chart.

John F Kennedy.

Draws a second male figure on the opposite side of the chart.

Sam Giancana.

Draws a female figure between the two male figures.

Judy Campbell.

Draws a line between JFK and Judy Campbell.

Jack Kennedy – Judy Campbell.

Draws a line between Sam Giancana and Judy Campbell.

Sam Giancana – Judy Cambell.

Draws lines between JFK and Sam Giancana.

Jack Kennedy – Sam Giancana. The President – Chicago Mob Don. The White House – the Mafia.

Draws a third male figure.

And the man responsible... Francis Albert Sinatra.

Song finishes.

No way was the President going to stay at Frank's estate. And it was bye-bye Judy.

DEAN: *(As JFK.)* Bye-bye, Judy.

JOEY: Frank...Frank... (*To audience – pointing to himself.*) Sam Giancana. (*Putting an arm around FRANK, as Sam Giancana.*) Frank, I'm getting a lot a harassment from your pal Bobby and the Justice Department.

FRANK: Gee, I'm sorry, Sam.

JOEY: (*As Giancana.*) I think it may be time for you to intercede.

FRANK: Intercede?

JOEY: (*As Giancana.*) You will recall how you indicated that my assistance in electoral matters would be recompensed with an easing of federal enquiries into certain activities?

FRANK: Sure I –

JOEY: (*As Giancana.*) Well, Frank, I'm gonna have to call in your marker. (*To audience – as himself.*) Frank's idea of dealing with it?… I'm Bobby Kennedy now – right.

FRANK scribbles something on a notepad and hands it to JOEY.

FRANK: This is my buddy.

JOEY: (*To audience – as himself, showing the note.*) 'Sam Giancana.'

FRANK: This is what I want you to know, Bob.

JOEY: (*To audience, as himself.*) The nerve of the guy! He gets nothin'. So now I'm Giancana again. (*To FRANK – as Giancana.*) Well…

FRANK: Thing is…

JOEY: (*As Giancana.*) Don't tell me you come back empty-handed.

FRANK: I can work it out. Just give me a little –

JOEY: (*As Giancana.*) Bullshit!

JOEY turns away from FRANK. He is joined by PETER, DEAN and SAMMY who play mob henchmen.

PETER: (*As henchman.*) I say we take him out.

SAMMY: (*As henchman.*) Yeh, let's show those Hollywood fruitcakes they can't get away with it. Let's hit Sinatra. Or I could whack out a couple of those other guys. Lawford and that Martin.

DEAN: (*As henchman.*) And I could take the nigger and put his other eye out.

JOEY: (*As Giancana.*) Paino, piano, piano. Take it easy. Shit, it's not Sinatra's fault the Kennedy's are assholes. But I tell you this, if I didn't like him, you can be goddamned sure he'd be a dead man. No, I got other plans for them guys.

PETER: (*As henchman.*) Other plans?

They break out of character.

JOEY: (*To audience.*) Like Villa Venice. Worked like this: Giancana sets up a mini-Las Vegas, north of Chicago – not that you could show he had any involvement, of course. Now, this was a real plush joint! Guests were greeted at the front entrance by gondoliers...

SAMMY poles DEAN across the stage in a gondola – the bar cart.

...who poled actual gondola through an actual river that snaked passed the Venetian Lounge and it's fine fountains into the main room. It seated eight hundred, and was sumptuously decorated with thick burgundy carpets, tasteful wall furnishings and tables dressed with fine linen and china.

FRANK: Dino, Sammy. How'd you like to play the Villa Venice?

DEAN: I dunno.

SAMMY: How much?

FRANK: For free.

JOEY: So, up roll Frank, Dean and Sammy. And the FBI get interested...

PETER and DEAN become FBI agents – they approach SAMMY.

PETER: (*As FBI agent.*) You're doing sixteen gigs in seven days?

SAMMY: That is correct. Can I get you guys a drink?

DEAN: (*As FBI agent.*) Thank you, sir, but we are on duty.

PETER: (*As FBI agent.*) And these gigs are for free?

SAMMY: For free.

DEAN: (*As FBI agent.*) Can you explain, sir, why you are doing free gigs instead of paying ones?

SAMMY: Baby, that's a good question. But I have to say it's for my friend Francis.

DEAN: (*As FBI agent.*) Or friends of his?

SAMMY: By all means.

PETER: (*As FBI agent.*) Friends like Sam Giancana?

SAMMY: By all means.

PETER: (*As FBI agent.*) And what does 'by all means' mean?

SAMMY: Baby, let me say this. I got one good eye, and that eye sees a lot of things that my brain tells me I shouldn't see. Because, if I do, my good eye might not be so good any more.

DEAN and PETER exchange a glance, then walk away.

JOEY: (*To audience.*) A month after opening, the Villa Venice closed. One day it burned to the ground. When they added it all together – the gig, the casino, the insurance – its shadow owner, Sam Giancana, was ahead three million dollars in cash: tax free. Frank had cleared his marker.

FRANK: All the creeps I'm supposed to have run with, all the thugs me, Dean and Sammy are supposed to have worked for, all the shit Peter Lawford was in on – guess who was the only one of us ever to testify at a Mob murder trial: Joey Bishop.

JOEY: All I had to do was testify I wasn't there.

FRANK: Yeh, yeh…

JOEY: So, Frank – tell me about that Cop.

FRANK: What cop?

JOEY: At the Cal Neva.

FRANK: Drop it, Charlie.

JOEY: Tell me.

FRANK: It was an accident.

JOEY: Did you take out a contract?

FRANK: Con– ? What are you talking about?

JOEY: I'm talking about that waitress you had a thing with. That deputy sheriff she just married.

FRANK: Joey, Joey, c'mon…

JOEY: Tell me what happened, Frank. Was it Giancana? I mean, I know we got up to some, but murder –

FRANK: Forget it.

JOEY: That's just it, Frank. I can't. (*To audience.*) In 1962 Frank and a coupla others decided to buy themselves into the Cal-Neva Lodge –

FRANK: Wo! Wo! Wo! What the hell you think you're doing, Charlie?

JOEY: I'm gonna tell this story, Frank. (*To audience.*) The big novelty about this place was that it straddled the state line. The rooms and restaurant were in California, the casino was in Nevada; the border ran right through this big outdoor swimming pool. But there was also a silent partner in Frank's enterprise – Sam Giancana. On the second night of the grand re-opening...

PETER strides up to FRANK. PETER is playing the Deputy Sheriff.

PETER: (*As Deputy.*) You know who I am?

FRANK: You're a cop.

PETER: (*As Deputy.*) I just got married.

FRANK: Congratulations.

PETER: (*As Deputy.*) She works here. Waitress.

FRANK: Well, that's marvellous.

PETER: (*As Deputy.*) You've been screwing her.

FRANK: Listen, buddy –

PETER: (*As Deputy.*) And it's gonna stop.

FRANK: Don't tell me –

They fight. It's nasty. PETER gets the better of FRANK and knocks him out. PETER walks off. FRANK comes round, feels his jaw.

JOEY: (*To audience.*) He couldn't finish the weekend's performances. He went into Reno, complained to the sheriff, who immediately suspended his deputy; two weeks later...

Sound of a car. PETER sits in the front seat. Something is wrong. The car swerves. Crash. Blackout. Lights back up.

(*To audience.*) The guy dies in a mysterious automobile accident not far from the hotel. No one sees what happened. (*Sings.*) Whoops there goes another problem, ker-pop!

FRANK: Enough!

JOEY: The guy hit you for schtupping his wife, Frank.

FRANK: I didn't kill him.

JOEY: So who did?

FRANK: It was an accident.

JOEY: On an empty road? In a new car?

FRANK: I hated that place.

JOEY: I wonder why. (*To audience.*) Prostitution. Shootings. Giancana in a fistfight. Monroe popping pills.

FRANK: I burned the photos.

JOEY: He burned the photos. What photos, Frank?

FRANK: Marilyn. I took a roll round the hotel. (*To 'Marilyn' in the audience.*) You remember? Coupla weeks later, when you died, I burned them.

DEAN: She was some broad.

SAMMY: Sure was.

JOEY: She was 'some broad'? She was dynamite – sleeping with the president, the attorney general, the nation's most popular singer; under surveillance by the FBI and the mob; strung out on drugs and rotten luck; with only a showbiz shrink and some guy name of Peter Lawford to keep her steady.

Music cue: 'Memories Are Made of This'.

Song: 'Memories Are Made of This'.

FRANK, DEAN, SAMMY and JOEY sing. Then they talk over the music.

DEAN: (*To PETER.*) So, Charlie, you ever…

PETER: No, I…you know.

DEAN: You never?

PETER: Nah. We rendezvoused, one time. At her place. But her living room…it…eurgh!

JOEY: It 'eurgh'?

PETER: On the carpet…all this chihuahua poop – it kinda put me off my stroke.

JOEY: (*To audience.*) She bugged her own home and began talking about using the tapes.

PETER: She made her last ever phone call to me. And you know…what she…what she said? She said: 'Say goodbye to yourself, because you're a nice guy.'

DEAN: Ahhhhhh…

PETER: And they…they made me the scapegoat, but I…No one ever blamed Jack or Bobby. I was only doing what they asked me to do.

DEAN sings alone.

Song finishes.

JOEY: Frank, what was the name of that film you made? One about the assassination of a US presidential candidate?

FRANK: The Manchurian Candidate. And before you say anything, I went straight to Jack with that, and he said he thought it would make a swell film. And I withdrew it from circulation when…when… And when I heard Lee Harvey Oswald had been a fan of another picture of mine I withdrew that too… I was all broke up.

JOEY: Yeh. You stopped filming for a whole half-hour when you heard Kennedy got shot.

FRANK: I was in shock!

SAMMY: It was one helluva time.

FRANK: (*To PETER.*) Why wasn't I invited?

PETER: Frank?

FRANK: To the funeral?

PETER: I... How do I know?

FRANK: You know!

PETER: I swear... I... Frank...

FRANK: Fuckin' English bum!

FRANK goes to mix himself a drink.

JOEY: (*To PETER – whispers.*) Why didn't they invite him?

PETER: (*Whispers.*) It just wasn't possible. He'd already been too much of an embarrassment to the family. You know, when I heard, I threw up all over the kitchen.

JOEY: I really wanted to know that.

SAMMY: Next thing: Dr King is murdered. Then Bobby. Man, the world gone crazy.

FRANK: That why you decided to come out for Nixon?

SAMMY: That why you came out for Ronald Regan for governor of California?

JOEY: That was a shock.

PETER: It figured.

FRANK: Yeh, yeh, But Nixon, Smokey. I mean, c'mon...

SAMMY: At least when Nixon invited me to the White House he didn't cancel.

FRANK: He used you, Smokey.

SAMMY: Baby, I was on top, I owned a piece of a casino and I broke bread with the President. Just like Frank Sinatra.

JOEY: And his wife left him. Just like Frank Sinatra.

SAMMY: You leave May out of this.

JOEY: (*As May.*) Sammy…

SAMMY: Y'know what I was thinking?

JOEY: (*As May.*) Sammy, there's something…

SAMMY: Why don't we do a weekly 'Sunday at Sammy's'?

JOEY: (*As May, angrily.*) Yeah! Why don't we!

SAMMY: Hey hey, baby…

JOEY: (*As May.*) I never see you. Your children never see you. And when we do, it's always, let's get some people round, let's have a party.

SAMMY: Baby, baby, I love you, you know that.

JOEY: (*As May.*) And I love you. But I hate our life.

SAMMY: You don't mean that.

JOEY: (*As May.*) I do.

SAMMY: Whatever happened to the Mary Movie Star I married?

JOEY: (*As May.*) I guess she'd rather be plain Mrs Sharlie Brown. (*As himself.*) And May upped and took the kids to LA.

Music cue: 'What Kind of Fool Am I?'

SAMMY sings.

Song finishes.

FRANK: Dean, let's get outta here, find some girls, have us a party...

DEAN ignores FRANK – he mixes himself a drink.

Dean!

DEAN continues to ignore FRANK.

DEAN: (*Singing to himself.*) I left my heart in Fran Sancisco (*Spoken.*) Think I'll have me a little bacon with this salad.

JOEY: When Dean didn't want to know... Dean, the President would like you –

DEAN: (*Practising golf swing.*) Sorry, I'll be in Atlantic City.

JOEY: Sam Giancana just called, he –

DEAN: (*Practising golf swing.*) I'd love to help, but I'm not feeling too good right now.

JOEY: There are two FBI guys waiting –

DEAN: (*Practising golf swing.*) Tell 'em I don't know nothing.

JOEY: Dean Martin: the man who knew more about nothing than any man I ever met. He didn't give a damn, didn't matter who it was.

DEAN: (*Practising golf swing.*) Fore!

They all watch DEAN's shot and pull faces as it goes way off course – a window smashes.

Music cue: 'Little Ol' Wine Drinker Me'.

Song: 'Little Ol' Wine Drinker Me'.

DEAN fixes himself another drink, pops some pills.

FRANK: Joey, I'm worried about Dean.

JOEY: Why's that, Frank?

FRANK: Look at him! He's drunk as a log. He's on pills. He's got the shakes. He hit a house!

DEAN sings. After a couple of verses he speaks.

DEAN: (*Spoken.*) They don't know how I do it.

FRANK: Who don't know how you do what?

DEAN: NBC. The folks at the studio. They spend all week rehearsing the show, I turn up Saturday to record it, no rehearsal and I'm word perfect. Sort of. They think I'm a genius. But what they don't know is I'm rehearsing it all the time. I got a tape in my car. When I'm playing golf I'm going over it in my head. What do you think of that?

FRANK: Any coffee over there?

DEAN sings again. Then.

JOEY: (*To audience.*) It was the news about Dean Junior, pushed him over the edge. He was killed when his Air National Guard Phantom smashed into Mount San Gorgonio near Palm Springs. Dean was devastated.

DEAN sings the final verse.

Song finishes.

(*To audience.*) When Howard Hughes bought the Sands Hotel –

FRANK: That bum!

JOEY: After a show one night in the Copa Room, Frank accompanies a couple of Apollo astronauts into the casino. He goes to the baccarat table and asks for credit – (*As Dealer.*) I'm sorry, Mr Sinatra. I have it on strict instructions from Mr Hughes. No credit.

FRANK: (*Trying to laugh it off – but seething.*) That Hughes, all the money he spent to buy this joint, and he's just as much of a tightwad as the old owners. Ha ha…

JOEY: (*To audience – as himself.*) Frank was seething.

FRANK: They dare…to deny me…credit!

FRANK goes crazy. He smashes, rips, destroys everything in sight.

I built this fuckin' hotel from a sandpile and before I'm through that's what it'll be again!

FRANK exits. A moment of respite as JOEY, DEAN, PETER and SAMMY wonder if the tantrum is over. Then FRANK bursts back on stage driving a baggage cart – the bar cart. Mayhem. The sound of shattering glass as FRANK drives the cart through a plate glass window, then runs off.

JOEY: (*To audience.*) So Frank signs with Caesar's Palace. But it doesn't work out – another ugly scene, the casino manager pulls a pistol on him. Frank walks. Next: a businessman who asks Frank and Dean to keep the racket down in the Polo Lounge winds up with his head smashed in with a telephone. Comedians Jackie Mason and Sheckey Greene who do bits about Frank get shot at, harassed on the phone, beaten up, hospitalised.

FRANK: I think you said enough.

JOEY: I think I said enough. Oh, except – you retired in '71. Then made a comeback. Then retired. Then made a comeback. Then –

FRANK: Why don't you tell 'em what happened to you? (*To audience.*) Joey Bishop hosted his own chat show. ABC put four million dollars into it. It limped along for two painful years. Then a disastrous sit-com. Next: a semi-regular on talkshows, quiz shows, bad TV series. Oh, occasionally he showed up in a movie or on TV talking about the golden days with Frank, Dean, Sammy and Peter. He even started writing to editors correcting their stories about the Summit.

PETER: That's enough, Frank.

FRANK: (*To audience.*) And my pal Peter the brother-in-Lawford. He brings a pick-up in a black micro-skirt to Bobby's funeral. He drinks when he's in hospital being treated for drinking. He gives cocaine to his son as a birthday present. And for sex he resorts to this thing called an Acujack, some kinda contraption he uses to give himself a pathetic little orgasm. His fourth and final wife leaves him in disgust. Game shows, Fantasy Island, 'nostalgia cruises'. He stops shaving, bathing, changing clothes or bed linen. Lives in an apartment strewn with cat shit –

PETER: Charlie... Don't, Charlie.

FRANK: You wanna take over? Tell the folks out there about your big comeback?

PETER: Frank, I –

FRANK: (*To audience.*) 1984, he gets tossed a career bone by old MGM pal, Liz Taylor – a few days work on a TV movie. Turns up on set mumbling to himself, hazy, in a weird fog. Passes out and gets the axe. Next –

PETER: I'll...let me... (*To audience.*) The day after I got axed from the movie I collapsed. I'd been in and out of hospital and rehab. My liver and kidneys had virtually shut down; I turned yellow, slipped in and out of comas. On December twenty-third I sat up in bed, drank champagne and laughed. The next day I went into spasm, blood spurting from my mouth, nose and ears. That was it.

PETER goes to the back of the stage and sits down.

JOEY: (*To audience.*) Frank's pal, Sam Giancana, hid in Mexico for ten years, then he got hustled back to the States. Soon after, he was found in his basement, head full of .22 slugs, sausage and beans still frying on the stove where the killer got him.

SAMMY: Guys! I got an idea! Let's get back together again, do some shows!

JOEY: (*To audience.*) You gotta realise, this is 1987. Dean and Frank are in their seventies. Sammy, ten years younger, has just had hip surgery.

DEAN: Why don't we just find a good bar?

FRANK: Smokey, let's do it. (*Taking SAMMY to one side.*) I think it would be great for Dean. Get him out. For that alone it would be worth doing.

JOEY: (*To audience.*) Forty dates in thirty cities, a full orchestra and tech crew. Big gigs, just like rock stars – fifteen to twenty thousand seaters. They held a press conference. (*As Journalist.*) So the 'Together Again Tour'…

DEAN: Is there any way we can call this off?

JOEY: (*As Journalist.*) What material you gonna do?

FRANK: It'll be spontaneous.

SAMMY: Scripts are boring.

JOEY: (*As Journalist.*) No scripts?

DEAN: That's like doing a Broadway play. Which I hate. We're happy to be doing this. What the hell.

JOEY: (*Breaking out of Journalist character.*) You weren't happy though, were you, Charlie

Music cue: Medley.

FRANK sings the first verse of 'You Make Me Feel So Young'.

Then SAMMY takes over, then DEAN. Then back to FRANK.

They take turns on the repeats and sing the final line in unison.

The music goes into 'Sway', which is DEAN's number. He sings.

Then into 'Hey There', which SAMMY sings. FRANK sings 'The Lady is a Tramp'. DEAN sings 'Everybody Loves Somebody'.

Then it's into 'Me And My Shadow'. SAMMY takes the first two lines. DEAN complains in between lines.

DEAN: (*Spoken.*) Will someone tell me why we're here?

FRANK, and then SAMMY too, sing the next few lines.

I wanna go home.

One line to FRANK, one to SAMMY. Then.

SAMMY: (*Spoken.*) How do you like sitting in the back of the bus, Dean?

FRANK: Loves it. (*He sings.*)

DEAN: I'm getting outta here.

FRANK sings.

JOEY: After one gig?

FRANK and SAMMY sing.

DEAN: I've had enough

SAMMY sings a line.

FRANK and SAMMY sing together.

JOEY: That why you went to Vegas?

SAMMY sings a line.

And opened on the Strip?

FRANK and SAMMY sing the final line together.

Medley finishes.

SAMMY has a coughing fit.

The cigarettes, Sammy, they're gonna get you. (*To audience.*) May Eighteenth, 1990. The lights on all the Strip's marquees are dimmed for ten minutes – the first time since JFK was killed. Sammy Davis is dead.

SAMMY looks at JOEY, then slowly makes his way to where PETER is sitting upstage.

Throat cancer.

DEAN quietly makes his way upstage to where PETER and SAMMY are sitting.

Dean never got over his son. He drifted off into himself, wandering in and out of restaurants and country clubs, talking to no one. Then, when everyone was eating Christmas dinner, he quietly slipped away.

Music cue: 'My Way'.

Frank… Do we have to?

FRANK: What choice do I have?

Song: 'My Way'. FRANK sings. The song builds to the big ending, and in the final instrumental, JOEY speaks.

JOEY: Frank was eighty. He put up a fight as long as he could, concerts, tours, benefits, records. But not without embarrassment: forgotten lyrics, lapses in stage patter, physical collapse. His heart – a few sensational medical incidents, then he retreated to seclusion to wait for it. In the end it was sheer exhaustion that forced him to give up – but there was no doubt he'd won.

FRANK sings the final line.

Song finishes.

FRANK retreats upstage to be with PETER, DEAN and SAMMY.

SAMMY: Hey, Charlie, what about you?

JOEY: Not yet. Hey, you hear they pulled down the Sands.

FRANK: Good.

JOEY: Last show in the Copa Room – a freebie: a girl singer with a lumpy ass, a Welsh comic, a fruity magician, a middle-aged slob singing Elvis songs and doing a striptease. Then – lights out and the dynamite. You guys just gonna sit there?

FRANK, DEAN, SAMMY and PETER come downstage to join JOEY.

FRANK: So now whatta we do?

SAMMY: Last number, Frank. Like we used to.

FRANK: You mean?

SAMMY: Dean?

DEAN: Yeh. Why not.

SAMMY: (*To MD.*) Have you a key note, sir?

Music cue: 'The Birth of the Blues'.

Song: 'The Birth of the Blues'. They all sing, taking a line each in turn. After 'from a jail', FRANK throws in.

FRANK: (*Spoken.*) You're telling me!

And they carry on singing.

FRANK and DEAN sing together.

Then FRANK, DEAN and SAMMY.

Then FRANK, DEAN, SAMMY and PETER.

Finally, all five are singing together for the finale.

Song finishes.

During the applause FRANK, DEAN, SAMMY and PETER exit. JOEY finishes taking the bow on his own. He looks around – everyone has gone.

JOEY: Guys…Get back out here!

JOEY looks at the audience. He steps back from the microphone. He looks off stage.

Guys… Guys…

JOEY looks at the audience. He's lost, confused. He looks off. A beat. Lights down.

The End.